The *SUPERPOWER* Field Guide

MOLES

BY RACHEL POLIQUIN

ILLUSTRATED BY
NICHOLAS JOHN FRITH

HOUGHTON MIFFLIN HARCOURT
Boston   New York

For my Rose and Hazel, small but mighty. —R.P.

To J.J.A. and H.B. Thanks for the inspiration. —N.J.F.

A special thank you to Dr. Kevin Campbell,
biology professor (University of Manitoba)
and ever-helpful mole expert.

Text copyright © 2019 by Rachel Poliquin
Illustrations copyright © 2019 by Nicholas John Frith

hmhbooks.com

The illustrations in this book were produced using a mixture of black ink,
pencil, and wax crayon on paper, in a technique known as "preseparation."
For printing purposes here, the artwork was colored digitally.

The text type was set in Adobe Caslon Pro.
The display type was set in Sign Painter House Showcard.

The Library of Congress has cataloged the hardcover edition as follows:
Names: Poliquin, Rachel, 1975– author. | Frith, Nicholas John, illustrator.
Title: Moles : the superpower field guide / by Rachel Poliquin ; illustrated
by Nicholas John Frith.
Description: Boston ; New York : Houghton Mifflin Harcourt, [2019] |
Series: Superpower field guide | Audience: Ages 7–10. | Audience: K to grade 3
Identifiers: LCCN 2018034807
Subjects: LCSH: Moles (Animals)—Juvenile literature.
Classification: LCC QL737.S76 P65 2019 | DDC 599.33/5—dc23
LC record available at https://lccn.loc.gov/2018034807

ISBN: 978-0-544-95107-5 hardcover
ISBN: 978-0-358-27259-5 paperback

Manufactured in China
SCP 10 9 8 7 6 5 4 3 2 1
4500794719

THIS IS A MOLE.

Just an ordinary mole.

But even ordinary moles are extraordinary. In fact, even ordinary moles are superheroes.

I know what you're thinking. You're thinking that moles are just squinty-eyed beasts that wreck your lawn with little mounds of dirt.

Well, you're right! And, believe it or not, those squinty eyes and mounds of dirt are proof that moles have superpowers.

You say, "Don't be ridiculous!"

I say, "You don't know moles."

But you will.

MEET ROSALIE

MEET ROSALIE, A COMMON MOLE. She may be small. She may be podgy. She may be almost blind. But never underestimate a humble hero like Rosalie! Her mole superpowers include:

ASTONISHING ARCHITECT OF DIRT

INDEFATIGABLE PAWS OF POWER
(That means paws that just won't quit.)

DOUBLE-THUMB-DIGGING DOMINANCE

ARMS OF HERCULES

SUPER-SQUIDGIBILITY

EARLY WHISKER WARNING SYSTEM

HEADLESS HOARDING

SALIVA OF DEATH (MAYBE?)

BLOOD OF THE GODS

Overlooked and out of sight, Rosalie has been toiling away at something wondrous. So sit back, relax, and allow me to tell you about the astonishing superpowers of **ROSALIE THE MOLE, BIONIC BURROWER!**

POTATO-SHAPELY

THE FIRST THING YOU NEED TO KNOW about Rosalie is that she is shaped like a potato. And not a new potato, all cute and round, but a plain old lumpy russet potato, the sort that sits in the bottom of your fridge, neglected and going a little spongy.

Of course, unlike potatoes, moles have fur, paws, and snouts. But just like potatoes, moles don't really have legs or necks or ears. (They have them, but they are too stubby to see.) So, if you imagine a potato growing fur and paws and getting pinched into a point at one end, you'll have yourself a mole.

Rosalie weighs three and a half ounces (100 grams). According to the Idaho Potato Commission, the average russet weighs twice as much. Yet Rosalie and the russet are both five inches long (12.7 centimeters), which means Rosalie is a lot lighter and squishier than a potato. Squishiness is an important mole fact. I'll come back to it later.

Now, potato-shapeliness is definitely too dowdy to be a superpower. But believe it or not, it's a **MOLE'S SECRET WEAPON.**

Let me explain.

Scientists say moles and potatoes have *cylindrical* bodies. *Cylindrical* is a fancy way of saying "shaped like a tube." But if you look at a potato, you'll notice it is not shaped *like* a tube so much as shaped *to fit inside* a tube. And that is the important thing about potato-shapeliness—it helps moles fit in tubes. A giraffe would not fit in a tube. Neither would a poodle, nor a chicken, nor any other animal with long legs and a long, bendy neck. Big floppy ears would also not be good in a tube. Take it from me, if you're going to live in a tube, it's best to be shaped like a potato.

Of course, moles don't live in any sort of tube. They live in underground tunnels. And not just any underground tunnel. Moles are **MASTERMINDS OF UNDERGROUND EXCAVATION!** They are **ASTONISHING ARCHITECTS OF DIRT!** They are **TUNNELING TORPEDOES!** Which brings me to **ROSALIE'S FIRST SUPERPOWER.**

EVERYBODY KNOWS MOLES DIG TUNNELS. But few people know just how astonishing mole tunnels are.

Lots of animals can dig tunnels from their front doors to their bedrooms. Maybe they'll dig another room for Auntie Susan or a hallway to a secret back door. But Rosalie didn't stop at one or two tunnels. She's dug a labyrinth of tunnels with hallways and highways, underpasses and roundabouts, sleeping chambers and storerooms like you've never imagined. She's even built herself a *fortress,* and I'm not trying to sound grand. That's actually what scientists call it.

HERE IS ROSALIE'S HOME.

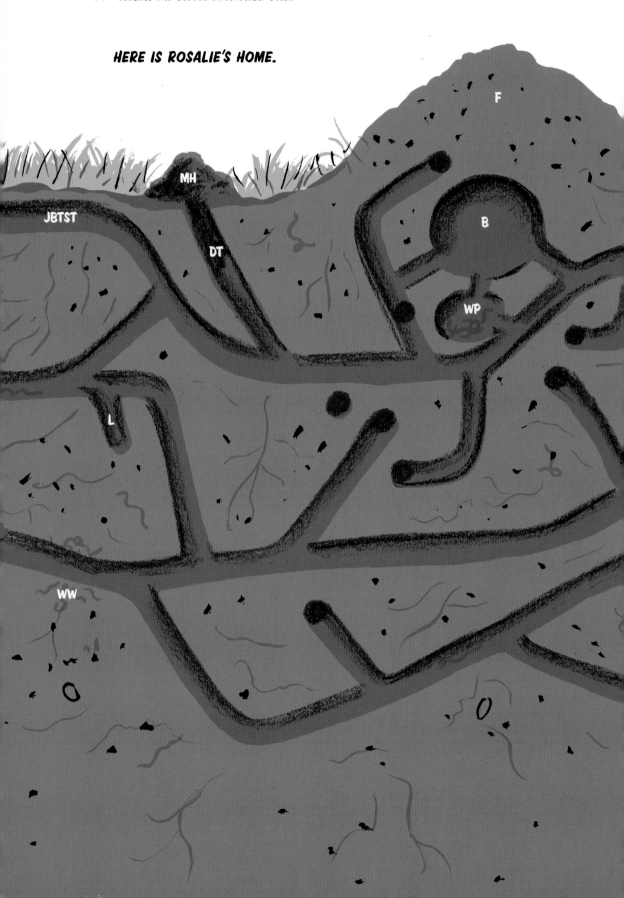

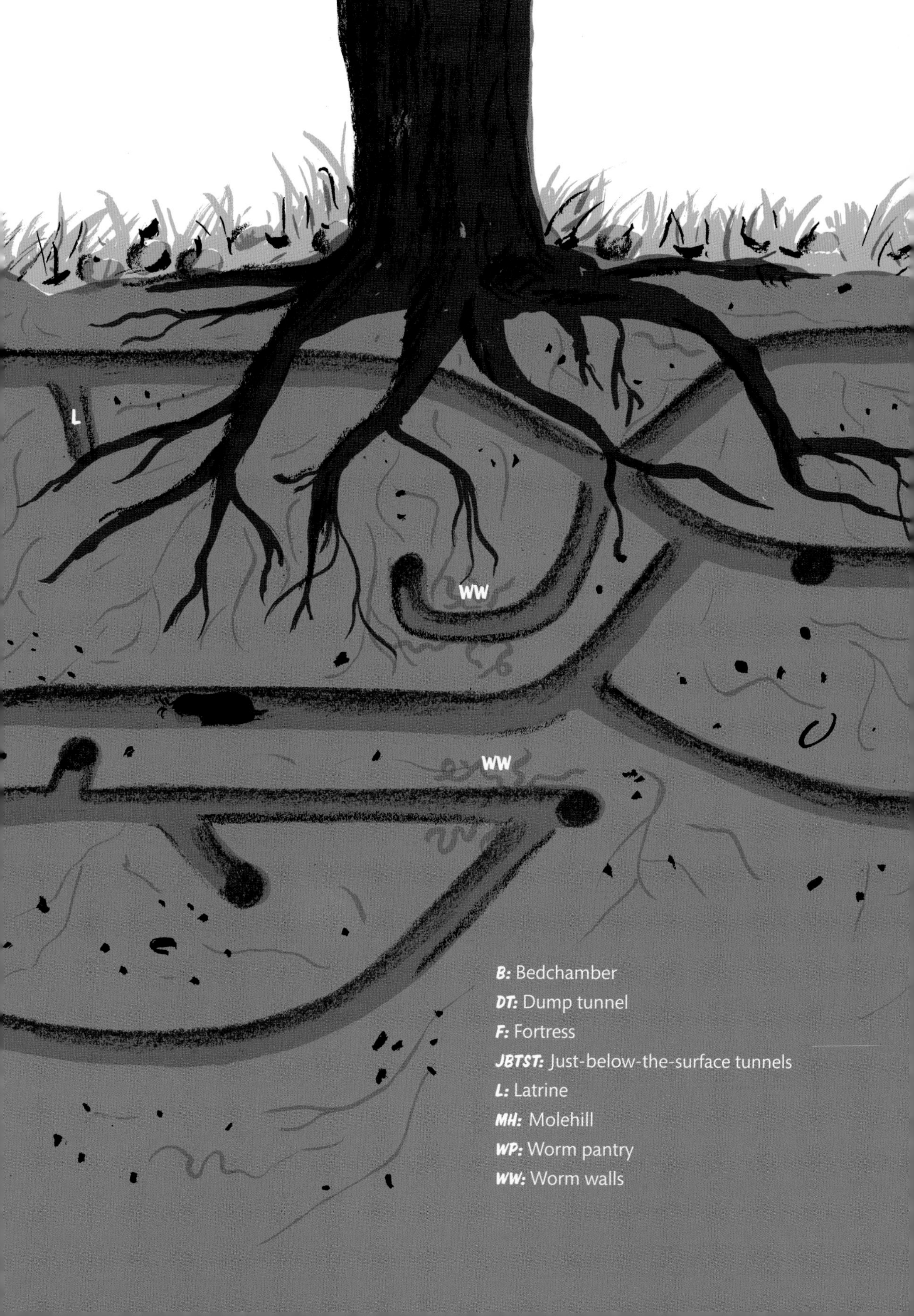

L

WW

WW

B: Bedchamber
DT: Dump tunnel
F: Fortress
JBTST: Just-below-the-surface tunnels
L: Latrine
MH: Molehill
WP: Worm pantry
WW: Worm walls

There's the fortress **(F)**. It's bigger than you'd think. I'm guessing it has over seven hundred and fifty pounds (340 kilograms) of soil! It has all sorts of tunnels running through it, and in the middle you can see Rosalie's bedchamber **(B)**.

Then there are at least eleven tunnels **(T)** running in all directions. They are about two inches (5 centimeters) wide, just wide enough for Rosalie to scamper through. As you can see, they are at different depths with various up routes and down routes and connecting passageways. It's a crazy network of tunnels down there! Some are more than five feet (1.5 meters) deep and run for hundreds of

Not all moles build fortresses, and scientists aren't exactly sure why certain moles do. Some scientists think all that dirt makes mole nests super-cozy, and sleeping aboveground is always a good idea in case the floods come.

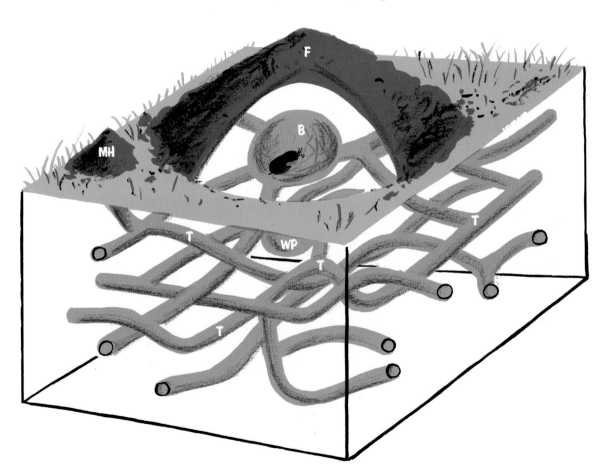

yards. These are Rosalie's permanent highways, and many have been around for years. Some were dug by her grandfather!

Then there are her just-below-the-surface tunnels **(JBTST)**. They're snack trails. They aren't built to last, but I'll explain that later. And I'll explain that slanting **DT** tunnel later too.

Next, the squiggly worm walls **(WW)** and the worm pantries **(WP)**. All I'll say about those for now is that they're one part clever, two parts crafty, and six parts gross. And speaking of gross, **L** is the *latrine*. As you might know, *latrine* is a polite word for "place to poop."

And, finally, Rosalie's molehills **(MH)**. Those piddly piles of dirt are all most people think moles can make! Can you believe it? And all the while, Rosalie has been excavating a **SECRETLY SUPERB SUBTERRANEAN SYSTEM OF SUPERHIGHWAYS** that can spread an acre or more underground. That's a football field's worth of tunnels!

Now, I'm sure you have a lot of questions, like *How does a spongy potato do all that?* And *Is a mole really a potato?* And *Why are we even talking about potatoes?* These are all very good questions. So let's get down to business and begin at the beginning: *How does a spongy potato do all that?*

Let's review what you already know about Rosalie:

1. She looks like a potato.
2. That potato can dig!

Don't be fooled by Rosalie's humpy-dumpy body. She may not be as fast as a speeding bullet. She may be spongy and small. But with all her superpowered digging parts put together, Rosalie is a **TUNNELING TORPEDO!** Let's start with those itsy-bitsy, teeny-weeny **INDEFATIGABLE PAWS OF POWER!**

MOST ANIMALS THAT DIG for a living have **PAWS OF POWER** with sharp claws. And so do moles. But mole paws are supercharged. First off, they're huge! If you had mole paws, your hands would be bigger than baseball mitts. They'd be giant, pink, wrinkly, extra-large baseball mitts. With claws.

Rosalie's paws are huge for her size, but they're itsy-bitsy compared to shovels, which is what you would need to dig tunnels. Each paw is about an inch (2.5 centimeters) wide—or about as big as the spoon your granny uses to stir her tea. Imagine digging any sort of tunnel through hard dirt with that spoon, let alone a football field of crisscrossing tunnels! That's what I call **INDEFATIGABLE PAWS OF POWER!** Admittedly, your granny's teaspoon is as blunt as a tennis shoe, and Rosalie's paws have fearsome claws that tear through dirt like blazing bitsy backhoes, but you get the idea.

GRANNY'S TEASPOON

MOLE PAW

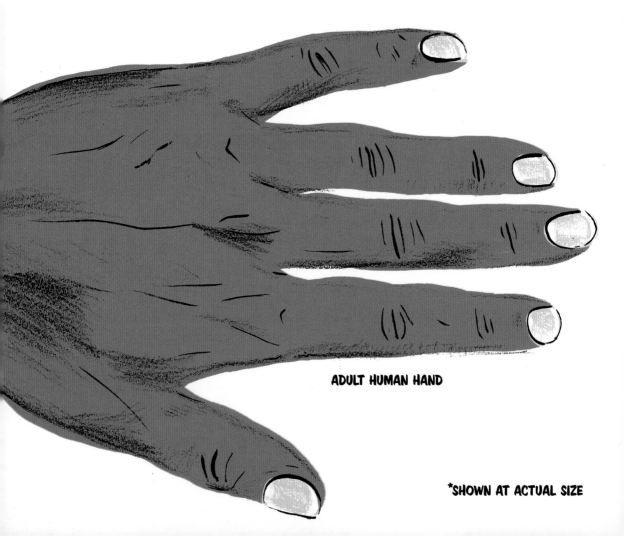

ADULT HUMAN HAND

*SHOWN AT ACTUAL SIZE

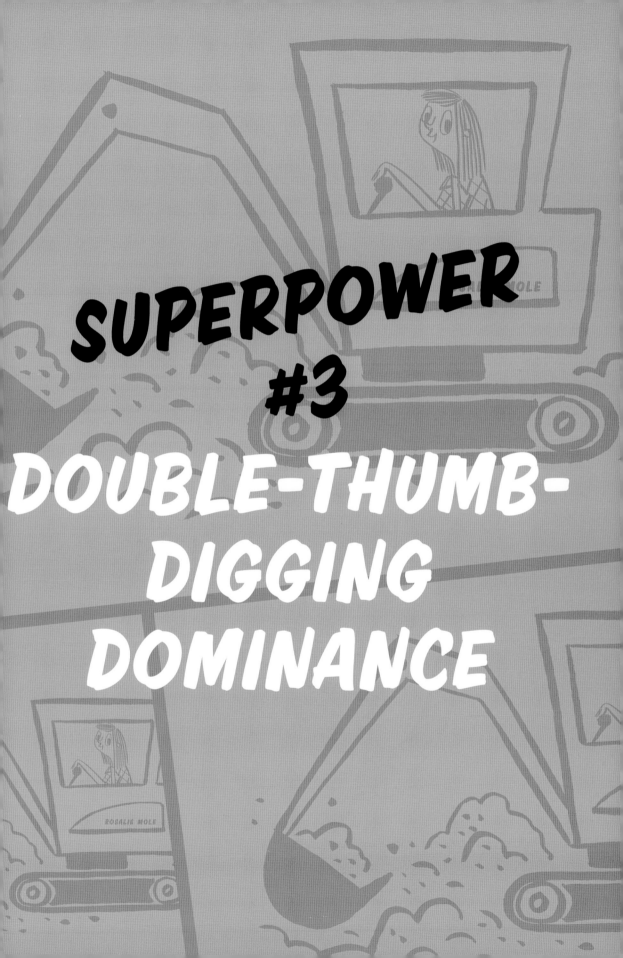

SUPERPOWER #3

DOUBLE-THUMB-
DIGGING
DOMINANCE

NEXT, MOLES HAVE SOMETHING no other digger has—an extra thumb on each paw. Sort of. It isn't really a thumb. It doesn't bend. It doesn't have a nail. You can't really tell it's there from the outside. But if you look at an x-ray of Rosalie's paw, you can see a weird, long, curvy bone has grown up from her wrist alongside her real thumb. Scientists call it a *prepollex,* but I call it a weird fake thumb, or WFT for short.

Why on earth would Rosalie have such a thing? Well, pretend for a moment you're a mole scrabbling through a dirt wall in front of your face.

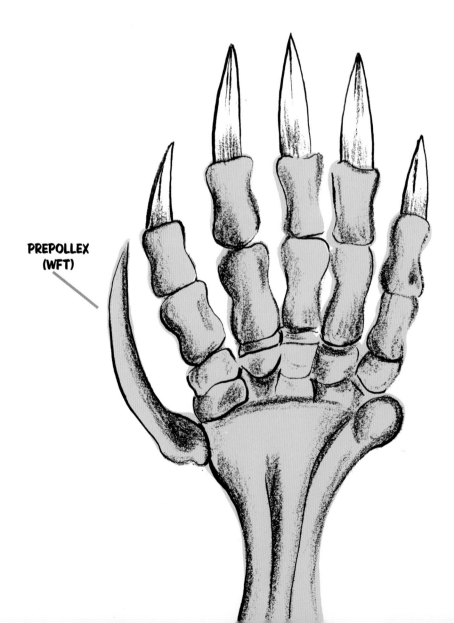

PREPOLLEX
(WFT)

Scrabble-scrabble.

Scrabble-scrabble.

Your fingers might be scrabbling, but what are your thumbs doing? I bet they're sticking out the sides, not doing much of anything. Thumbs are really useful for opening jars and holding pencils, but they aren't as good as fingers for scratching dirt.

Did you ask, "Why have two useless things—or four, if you count both thumbs on each front paw—when one useless thing is usually more than enough?"

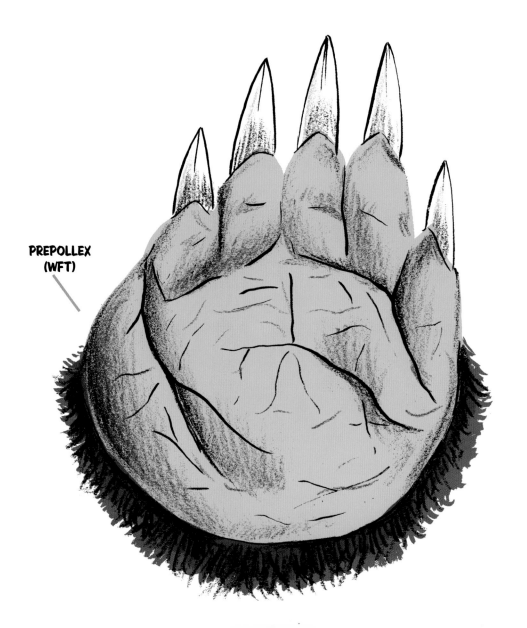

PREPOLLEX
(WFT)

This is a very good question. And here is my best answer.

Neither Rosalie's real thumbs nor her WFTs actually work like thumbs. First off, her real thumbs are more like fingers. Look at your hand—see how your thumb sticks out to the side? It's what makes your thumbs special and especially good for holding pencils. Scientists call such thumbs *opposable.* Now look at Rosalie's paw. It's hard to tell which finger is a thumb. You can only tell which is what because her palm is fatter on the thumb side. That palm bulge is her WFT, and it's another secret mole strength.

As you can see, it makes Rosalie's paw wider, and, a bigger shovel is always good. The bone also makes her paw super-strong and super-stiff along the edge, which supercharges her dirt-digging. That's what I call **DOUBLE-THUMB-DIGGING DOMINANCE!**

Now, just because you have a big shovel does not mean you can lift it. And the same goes for Rosalie's paws—we need to give those paws some power!

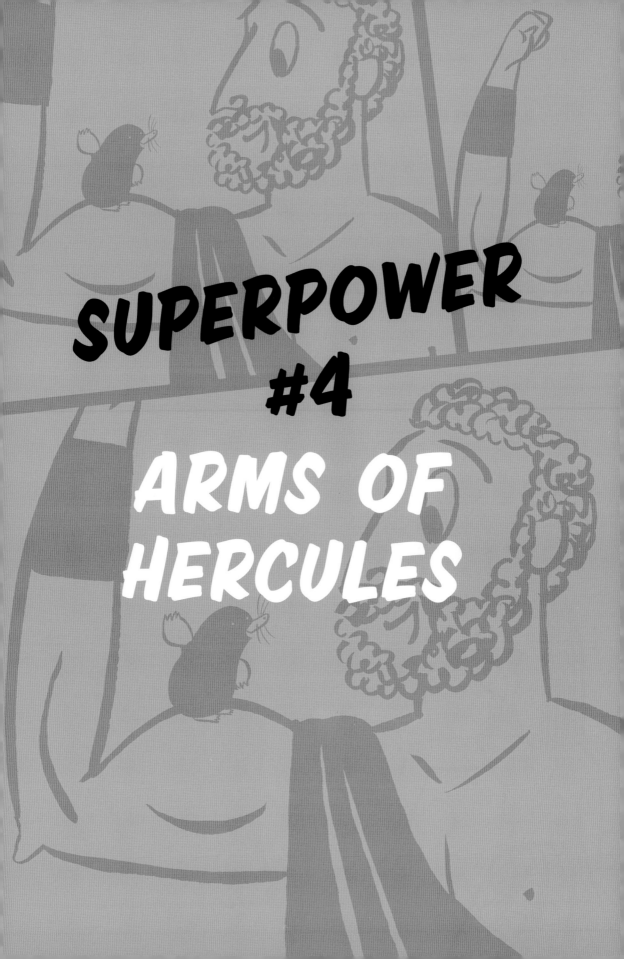

SUPERPOWER #4

ARMS OF HERCULES

HAVE YOU EVER SEEN PICTURES OF HERCULES, flexing his big arms and lifting a bull above his head? It's very impressive. But you know what? *Rosalie would be stronger than Hercules . . .* if Hercules were potato-size.

Rosalie has supersize paws and extra thumbs, but she gets her super-strength from her arm bones, which are the weirdest arm bones in the world. In fact, Rosalie's arm bones might be the weirdest bones ever seen. By anyone. Ever.

Don't believe me? Have a look for yourself.

Here we have the upper arm bone of a cow, a human, a bat, and a mole.

Your upper arm bone is officially called a ***humerus,*** and it connects at the top with your shoulder and at the bottom with your elbow. Animals come in all shapes and sizes, and so do humeri. (*Humeri* is the plural of *humerus.* It rhymes with *samurai.* And while we're on the subject, *humerus* is pronounced exactly like *humorous,* which is appropriate because Rosalie's humerus is pretty funny-looking.)

**CAN YOU SPOT THE ONE
THAT DOESN'T BELONG?**

HUMERUS

HUMAN   COW

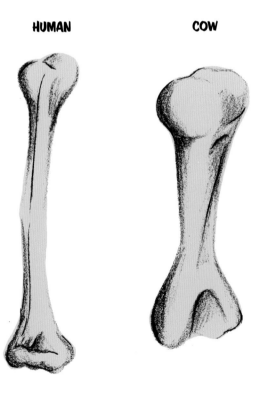

Heavy animals that walk on all fours, like cows, have thick bones and big connecting knobs at the top and bottom of their bones for strong muscle attachments. Because we humans use our arms for waving and hugging rather than walking, we have slender arm bones with smaller connecting knobs. Bats need strong but lightweight bones for flying. Their arm bones are particularly graceful. And then there's the mole humerus.

I don't even know how to describe it. It looks like a tooth, maybe? Or a gear? Or like a pancake with two big bites taken out of it? In any case, it definitely does not look like an arm bone. But it is.

Those big bite marks are where Rosalie's arm muscles attach. The big gaps and pointy bits allow for the large and strong muscle attachments that give Rosalie her Herculean strength. And she needs it. Digging is the hardest work around. Digging takes more muscles and uses more energy than running, swimming, or even flying!

BAT   MOLE

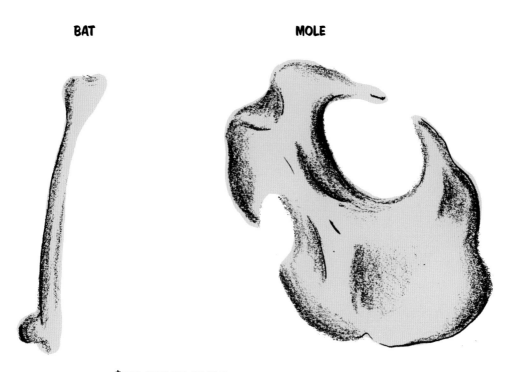

*ART NOT TO SCALE

How strong is she? Well, for every yard or so (1 meter) of tunnel she digs, Rosalie has to remove about four and a half pounds (2 kilograms) of soil. So if Rosalie digs sixty-five feet (20 meters) in a day, she'll move four hundred times her weight in dirt. She can move her own weight in dirt every minute! She can push thirty times her weight *uphill!* Now, numbers are just numbers, so let me explain how strong Rosalie really is by comparing her to Hercules and his bull.

Let's say Hercules weighs four hundred pounds (181 kilograms). So, if Hercules lifted thirty times his weight, he would heave not one bull, not two bulls, but eight bulls above his head! Impossible! I don't even think Hercules's dad, the King of Thunderbolts, Mr. Zeus himself, could do it. But Rosalie can.

Okay. Time to put all her superpowered digging parts together.

HOW TO DIG LIKE A TUNNELING TORPEDO

THERE ARE LOTS OF DIGGERS in the world. Gophers dig. Beavers dig. Rabbits and armadillos dig. Even your dog can dig a hole. But nobody digs with the flair and finesse of a mole.

Most animals just scratch and scrabble with their front paws while dirt sprays out behind them. What a mess! Rosalie is far more elegant. Instead of scrabbling, she swims!

In loose soil, like a vegetable garden, Rosalie does the breaststroke. See how her front paws are turned so that her palms face outward? When she digs, her big humeri work like massive levers, scooping her forepaws through the earth and pushing dirt backwards, just like you when you do the breaststroke. This is how she digs her just-below-the-surface tunnels—you can actually see the ridge forming above her as she digs. If she hits the roots of a lettuce, she'll knock the lettuce down and keep on going.

In deeper soil, Rosalie does a one-arm crawl. While her right forepaw digs, she steadies herself against the sides of the tunnel with her left forepaw and her two back feet. As she scoops dirt backwards with her right paw, her right hind foot kicks it behind her. After three scoops, she'll change paws to use her left forepaw to dig and her left leg to kick.

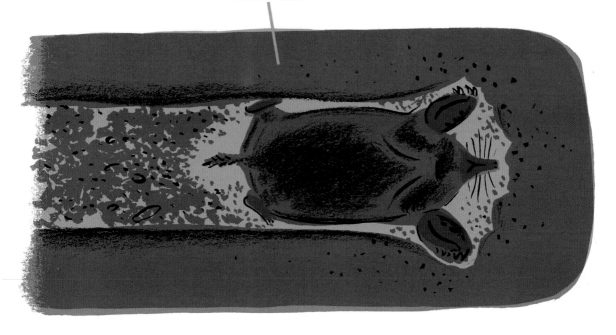

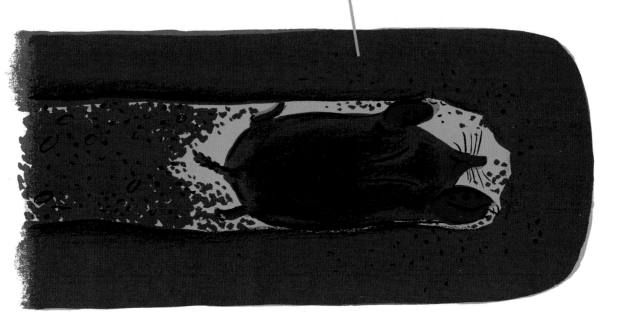

But Rosalie has two big problems.

PROBLEM #1: What to do with all that dirt? When your dog digs a hole, he sprays dirt everywhere. If Rosalie did that, she'd plug her tunnels behind her as fast as she dug them in front. And that wouldn't be smart. In fact, it would be very, very unsmart.

PROBLEM #2: If Rosalie digs tunnels just wide enough for her potato-shaped body, how does she turn around? Does she just keep digging in circles, leaving a spray of dirt behind her?

Of course not. Rosalie solves both problems with a gobsmackingly squishy superpower.

SUPERPOWER #5

SUPER-SQUIDGIBILITY

REMEMBER WHEN I SAID THAT MOLES were a lot squishier than potatoes and that mole squishiness was an important mole fact? Well, now you know why. If Rosalie were firm like a potato, she would never be able to turn around in her tunnels.

SUPER-SQUIDGIBILITY to the rescue!

With slender hips and a super-flexible spine, Rosalie can fold her body in half and do a somersault through her hind legs!

So that's problem #2 solved. And because she can turn in tight tunnels, she also has problem #1 solved.

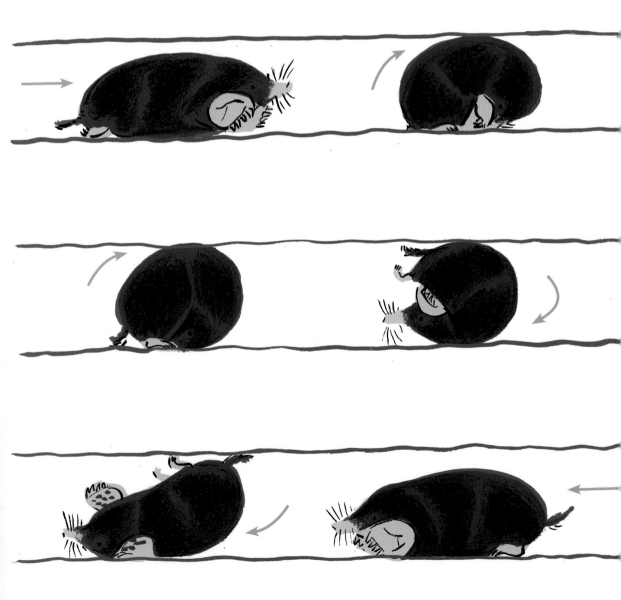

You see, Rosalie makes special dirt-dumping tunnels to get rid of the dirt. I call these **DUMP TUNNELS,** but their proper name is **LATERAL SHAFTS.** If you turn back to the map of Rosalie's home on page 14, you can see the dump tunnel **(DT)** runs at a 45-degree angle from a main highway up to the surface. And do you see what is on top of that dump tunnel . . . a molehill! Molehills aren't doors to the outside world—they are dirt dumps!

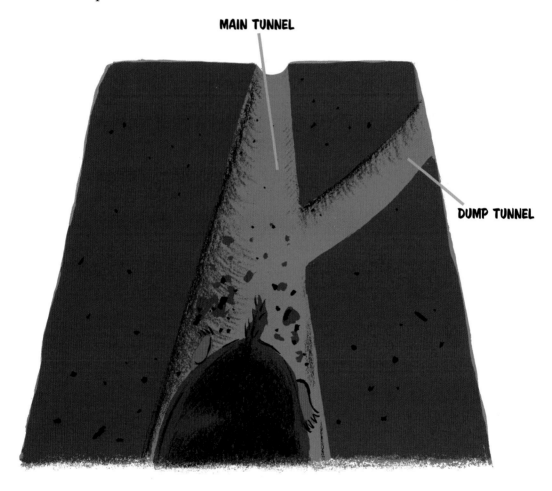

MAIN TUNNEL

DUMP TUNNEL

But here's the snag: dump tunnels are always behind Rosalie as she digs new tunnels in front of her. This might be a problem for a potato. But not for Rosalie!

So let's watch as Rosalie puts her **SUPER-SQUIDGIBILITY** into super-tunneling action.

STEP 1: Once she has dug a good load of dirt, she does a somersault.

STEP 2: She begins pushing the dirt back down the tunnel.

STEP 3: She keeps pushing and pushing until she comes to the closest dump tunnel. Then she heaves the dirt up. (Egads. That's hard work.)

STEP 4: And with one final heave, she pushes the dirt out the hole.

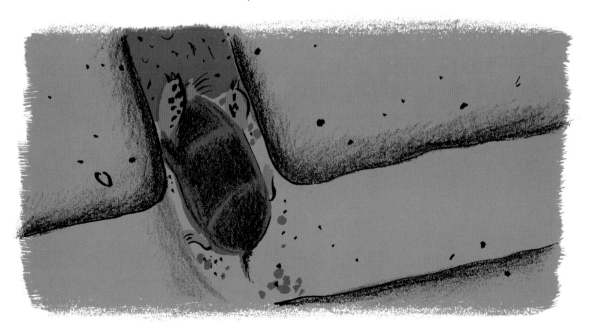

STEP 5: Ta-da! A molehill! Cute, isn't it?

Then back to digging, another somersault, and more pushing.

Dig, somersault, push.

Dig, somersault, push.

It's serious work keeping your tunnels tidy. Soon the dump tunnel is plugged. But by now, Rosalie has dug far enough down her tunnel that it's time to dig a new dirt dump anyway.

That's why molehills are often evenly spaced across your lawn. How shipshape! How tidy!

It takes mining engineers years of school to figure such things out, but Rosalie does it with her eyes closed, literally. If her eyes were open, she'd need dirt goggles.

Phew! That was a lot of information. **TIME FOR YOUR FIRST QUIZ.**

QUIZ #1

PLEASE ANSWER TRUE OR FALSE.

1. The word *mole* comes from the Old English word for "He Who Hurls the Earth."

2. Moles are strong enough to juggle bulls.

3. The best way to get rid of a pesky mole is to plug her molehills with potatoes.

4. When Auntie Susan comes for a visit, she always sleeps in Rosalie's bed.

5. You might have heard the saying "Don't make a mountain out of a molehill." It means don't make a big fuss over a little problem. Now, even though molehills aren't as big as mountains, they can still kill kings!

1. **TRUE.** The word *mole* is short for the Old English word **mouldywarp**, which comes from the words *mould*, or soil, and *warp*, to throw. So *mouldywarp* basically means "dirt thrower," or "He Who Hurls the Earth," if you want to be dramatic.

2. **FALSE.** That's silly. I never said such a thing.

3. **FALSE.** But it is true that lawn-lovers hate seeing molehills polka-dotting their lawns and have invented all sorts of mean tricks to get rid of moles. Some use traps or poisoned worms, which are pretty awful. Others stick prickly brambles down tunnels or use noise machines to drive moles crazy. Still others try to stink moles out with rotting fish or weasel pee. Nasty!

4. **FALSE.** Auntie Susan is never invited for a visit. And even if Rosalie did invite her, she would never come. Moles are solitary creatures, which means they don't like visiting, and they don't like visitors. Plus, female moles *really* don't like each other. If Rosalie and Auntie Susan ever met, they might fight . . . to the death! I've heard that male moles are a tad friendlier.

5. **TRUE.** Can you believe it? A mole once killed a king! You see, back in 1702, William III, the king of England, was riding his horse across a lovely park when his horse stumbled on a molehill. William was thrown, and he died from his injuries two weeks later. Maybe that mole was Rosalie's great-great-great-great-great-grandfather. Who knows? In any case, time to meet the family.

KNOW YOUR MOLES

THE MOST IMPORTANT THING TO KNOW ABOUT MOLES

is that not all moles are actually moles. In fact, even if scientists call something a mole, it still might not be a mole.

You see, there are moles, golden moles, marsupial moles, shrew moles, shrew-*like* moles (that's actually their name), and mole rats, some of which are famously naked and among the scariest animals you'll ever see. For the most part, all these so-called moles are potato-shapely diggers with bad eyesight. But they are not all moles. Only moles, shrew moles, and shrew-like moles are true moles. All true moles are officially part of the Talpidae family (*talpid* is Latin for "mole"), and the last time I counted, there were forty-five species. (Scientists are not 100 percent sure how many mole species are living in the world. Some mole experts say there could be over fifty-five!)

The Talpidae family has three main branches: **NEW WORLD MOLES, OLD WORLD MOLES,** and the **ASIAN SHREW-LIKE MOLES.**

NEW WORLD MOLES live in North America. My favorites are the hairy-tailed mole and the star-nosed mole. We'll meet a star-nosed mole later. His name is Victor. He's a fun guy.

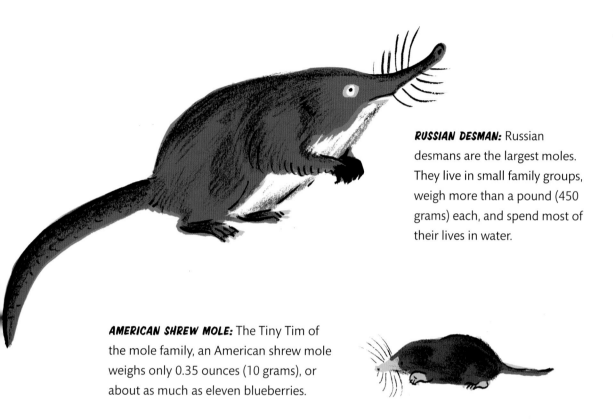

RUSSIAN DESMAN: Russian desmans are the largest moles. They live in small family groups, weigh more than a pound (450 grams) each, and spend most of their lives in water.

AMERICAN SHREW MOLE: The Tiny Tim of the mole family, an American shrew mole weighs only 0.35 ounces (10 grams), or about as much as eleven blueberries.

STAR-NOSED MOLE: One of the mole species that prefer life outside a tunnel. They love to swim! And yes, I will explain that thing on its nose.

MEDITERRANEAN MOLE: Also known as the blind mole, the Mediterranean mole has eyes, but its eyelids don't open.

Then there are the **OLD WORLD MOLES.** They live in Europe and Asia, and there's a lot of them. There is the European mole (often called the common mole), the Mediterranean mole, the Spanish mole, the Roman mole, the Himalayan mole, and the Japanese mountain mole. There is also the short-faced mole, the long-nosed mole, and the small-toothed mole. The shrew moles are also part of the Old World mole family. And apparently so are desmans—even though they have mini–elephant trunks and weird fat tails.

And, finally, the **ASIAN SHREW-LIKE MOLES,** which look more like shrews than moles, but scientists say they are more mole than shrew, so I guess they must be.

It's all a bit confusing. But the important thing to know is that Rosalie is a common European mole, and she lives under an apple orchard overlooking the sea somewhere in Wales.

I know New World animals are supposed to
live in the Americas, and Old World animals are
supposed to live in Europe and Asia. But moles
get a few things mixed up. The gansu mole is
a New World mole that lives in China, and the
American shrew mole is an Old World mole that
lives in America. Don't ask me why. Perhaps they
were switched at birth.

LIFE IN THE DARK

LIVING UNDER AN APPLE ORCHARD overlooking the sea sounds very pleasant, but the truth is Rosalie has probably never seen an apple, and she certainly can't see the sea.

People like to say that moles are blind, or, worse, that they don't have eyes at all! This isn't true. Moles do have eyes. They are tiny and hidden beneath their fur, but they are most definitely there. But it is true that moles have poor eyesight. They can tell darkness from daylight and probably see motion in bright light, but that's about it. Then again, that's all Rosalie needs.

You see, it's dark down there in her tunnels. Really, really dark. And Rosalie doesn't have tiny flaming torches on her tunnel walls. And she doesn't have a flashlight. Rosalie lives in a world of complete pitch-black darkness. Lots of aboveground animals, like owls and tarsiers, have huge eyes to see at night. But owls and tarsiers also have the moon and stars to light their way. Rosalie doesn't. Moonbeams don't shine underground. Even if she had enormous eyes, she still wouldn't be able to see a darn thing down there.

But don't feel sorry for Rosalie. She has other super-extraordinary powers that make even the sharpest eyesight unnecessary.

First up, Rosalie's *EARLY WHISKER WARNING SYSTEM.*

SUPERPOWER #6

EARLY WHISKER WARNING SYSTEM

HAVE YOU EVER WAITED FOR a train on a subway platform? Before you see the train in the tunnel, before you even hear it clattering down the tracks, you know it's coming because everything starts to shake and rumble. You can feel the train through your boots!

Now, imagine that it's a worm, not a train, coming through the tunnel. As the worm pushes along, every wormy wriggle causes the earth to vibrate just the tiniest bit, just like the train rumbling down the track. But worms are so small, and they move so slowly, those vibrations are very, very, very, very, very, very, very, very, very, very small. You're not going to feel anything through your boots unless your boots have whiskers.

Whiskers?

Did I just say that?

Yes, I did!

Rosalie doesn't have whiskers on her boots because she doesn't wear boots. But she does have an **EARLY WHISKER WARNING SYSTEM,** which lets her know everything that's happening in her tunnel.

You're probably thinking, *But whiskers can't be superpowers! My dog has whiskers. Uncle Tony's gerbil has whiskers.* This is true. Whiskers are ubiquitous (which means they are here, there, and everywhere), but that doesn't mean whiskers aren't amazing. I mean, have you ever really thought about whiskers? Do you even know what a whisker is?

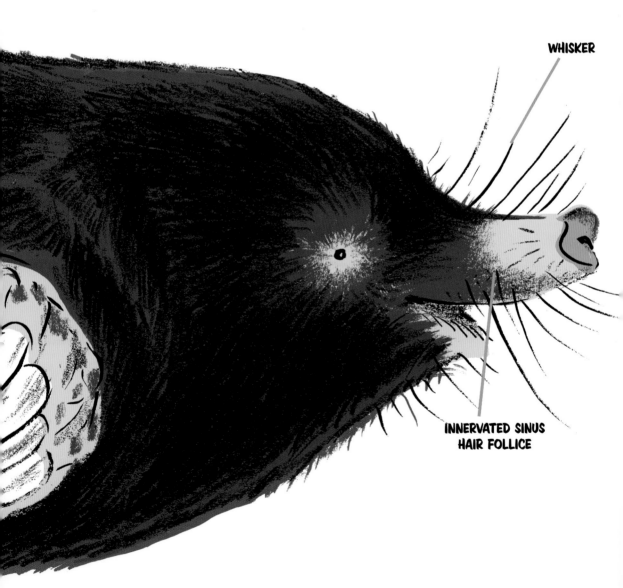

WHISKER

INNERVATED SINUS
HAIR FOLLICE

Yes, a whisker is a hair, but it's a very special kind of hair.

First, whiskers are thicker than normal hairs, and they're stiff, like wires, so they don't bend but flick when touched. More important, whiskers aren't just stuck in skin, like the hairs on your head. Each whisker is rooted in a wobbly sack of fluid, sort of like a tiny plastic bag of Jell-O.

So, imagine a stiff wire sticking out of a tiny bag of Jell-O. If you touch the wire, even ever so gently, you know the Jell-O bag will wibble and wobble all over the place. In fact, the Jell-O bag will (and pardon the big word) *amplify* the wire's movement. And that's how whiskers work. When Rosalie's whiskers touch something, the whiskers wiggle, their little sacks wiggle *even more* (that's what *amplify* means), and wiggly messages get sent to Rosalie's brain.

Scientists call the Jell-O bags ***INNERVATED SINUS HAIR FOLLICLES,*** which is just a fancy way of saying each Jell-O bag is filled with supersensitive nerves.

Rosalie's whiskers can pick up the smallest vibrations through the walls of her tunnels. From the slightest whisker twitch, Rosalie knows a worm is above her. And not only that, she knows how far above her it is, how big it is, what direction it's moving, how fast it's going, and whether it's smoking a cigar. (Just kidding about the cigar.)

More whiskers mean more information, and Rosalie is covered in them. She has whiskers on her chin, under her chin, and on her muzzle. She has tufts of whiskers on the sides of her face. She has whiskers on her forepaws. She even has whiskers on her tail! Now that's what I call a 360-degree ***EARLY WHISKER WARNING SYSTEM!***

Impressive, right? But wait till you hear what Rosalie's snout can do!

A NOSE THAT KNOWS

ROSALIE'S SNOUT IS LONG, HAIRLESS, AND TWITCHY. It looks like an ordinary snout, but don't be fooled. This is no ordinary nose! Sure, it's an ultrasensitive sniffing machine. But its secret superpower is not its sniffing supremacy. What if I told you Rosalie's nose is also a finger? Crazy, right?

Of course, Rosalie's nose is not *actually* a finger, but it sure acts like one. And you'll need a microscope to understand why.

If you look at Rosalie's snout under your microscope, you'll see its skin is covered with thousands of tiny bumps that look like the smallest cobblestoned street.

The bumps are known as **Eimer's organs,** and each one is connected to a network of nerves. When a bump touches something, it quivers and quavers and sends a message to Rosalie's brain, just like when your finger touches something.

EIMER'S ORGANS

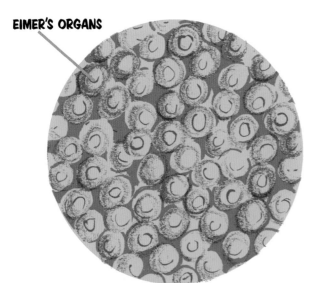

In the pitch-blackness of her tunnels, Rosalie's touchy-feely snout works just like a hungry finger, constantly twitching and poking and feeling around in the darkness for something yummy to eat. Big juicy earthworms are her favorite, but **grubs,** bugs, and beetles are just fine too.

Rosalie's snout finger is well worthy of being a superpower, but mole snouts get much, much better. What if I told you Rosalie had a hungry hand on her nose instead of just one finger? What if her nose had four hands with twenty-two fingers, all constantly touching and poking about for food? And what if those twenty-two fingers moved at supersonic speeds, faster than the eye can see?

Well, there is no *what if*. It's true! Except those supersonic snout fingers don't belong to Rosalie. They belong to her cousin Victor the star-nosed mole.

I know this is a book about Rosalie, but Victor's snout is one of the wonders of the animal kingdom. It is the nose of noses! **THE LIGHTNING GOD OF SNOUTS!** I just couldn't write a book about moles without talking about it. Prepare to be wowed!

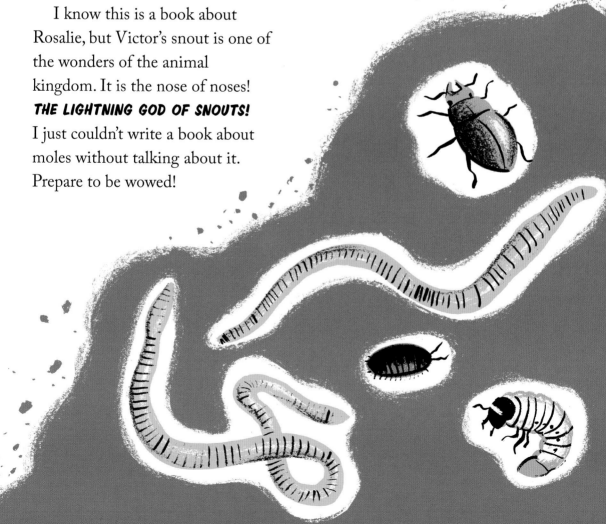

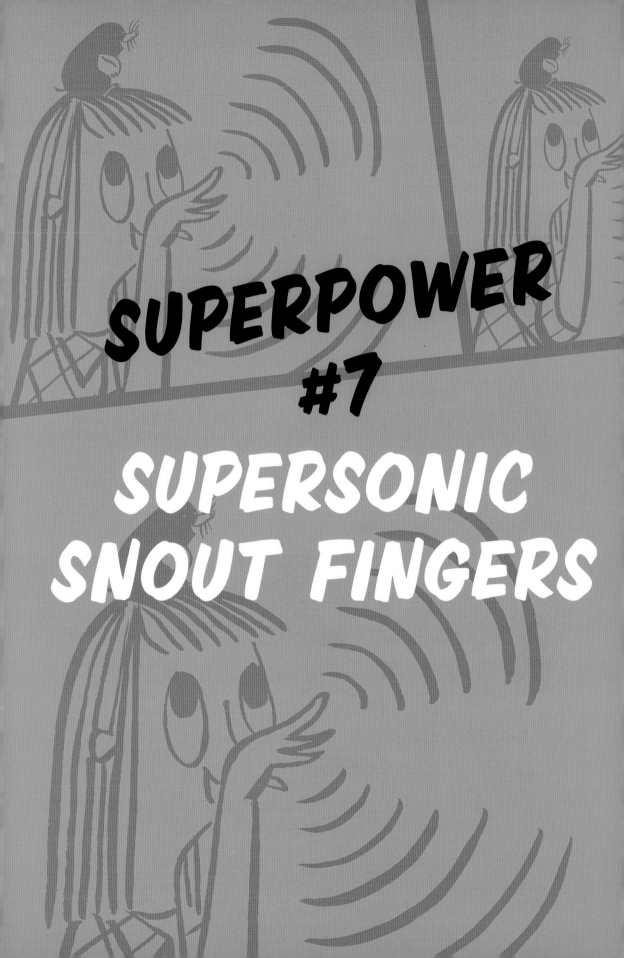

MEET VICTOR THE STAR-NOSED MOLE. He lives on the other side of the Atlantic Ocean from Rosalie, in a boggy corner of North Woods, Maine, in the United States of America.

As you can see, the cousins look very much alike. Victor is a bit smaller than Rosalie, and he has a long tail. But they both have **INDEFATIGABLE PAWS OF POWER.** You could easily mistake Rosalie for Victor if it weren't for that thing on Victor's nose.

Even Rosalie doesn't know what it is. If she could write a letter to Victor (which you know she can't, because of her thumbs), she would say something like this:

(I told you moles weren't a friendly bunch.)

Victor's star is made up of twenty-two fleshy rays, or what I like to call **SNOUT FINGERS.** Each fleshy ray is covered in thousands of tiny Eimer's organs, just like Rosalie has on her nose. Rosalie's snout has about two thousand Eimer's organs. That's a lot! But Victor's star has twenty-five thousand connected to more than one hundred thousand large nerve fibers. Your whole hand has only about seventeen thousand of these nerves. Imagine six times the sensitivity of your entire hand in the tip of your pinkie finger!

> More than half of Victor's brain is used to understand the information his star gathers.

Scientists have numbered the star's rays from 1 to 11 on each side. The two number 11s at the bottom are the stubbiest, but they are also the most important. The number 11s *always* poke anything Victor eats before he eats it, just to make double-sure it's a tasty treat and not something like an eraser or a shoe.

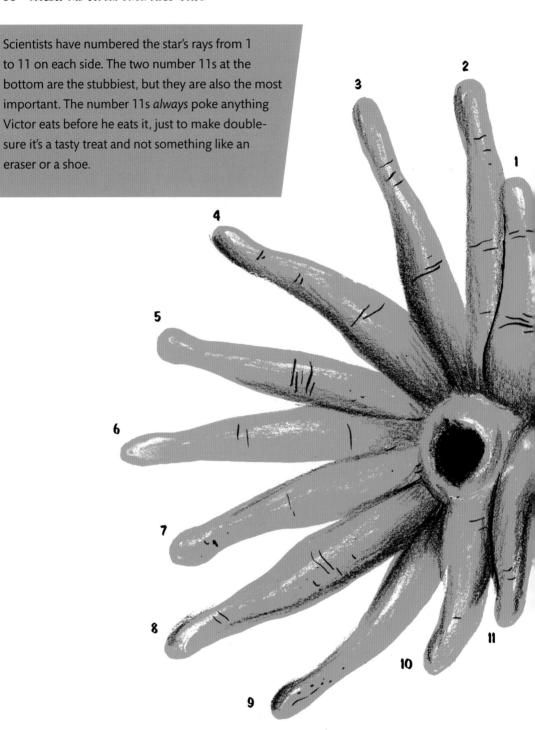

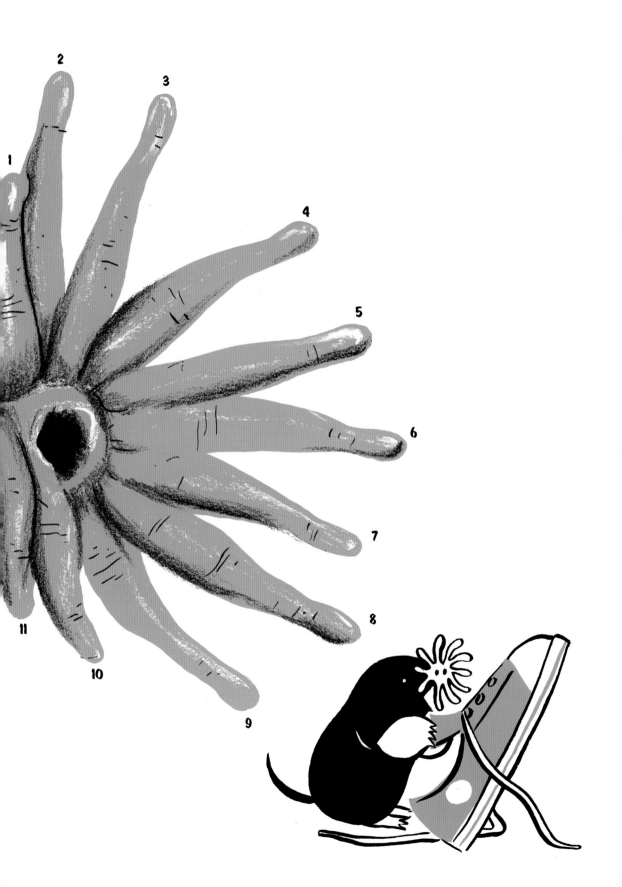

But hold on to your eyebrows, boys and girls, because it's time to explain the **SUPERSONIC MAGIC OF VICTOR'S SNOUT.**

When Victor called Rosalie's nose lazy, he was right. Victor and his snout hold the Guinness World Record for the fastest-eating mammal.

You see, Victor's star is always twitching and touching everything it can, as fast as it can. His star can touch thirteen things per second! Try drumming your fingers that fast. Victor can find, poke, poke, poke again, and eat a grub in as little as 0.12 seconds. That's faster than you can blink!

The faster Victor's snout moves, the faster he finds his next snack. Let's say your mother forgets to put away her box of chocolates and leaves it on the coffee table. How long does it take you to choose one, grab it, and eat it? Five seconds? Maybe four? You'd better do it quick, before your mother comes back. Well, in four seconds, Victor could have eaten the entire box and would be looking for more—if he liked chocolates, which he doesn't, so that's a bad example. What Victor does like are worms, bugs, and tiny larvae that live in boggy ground.

Are you thinking what I'm thinking?

What I'm thinking is this: *Sure, worms and tiny wiggly things move faster than chocolates, but still, wiggly things are not famous for their getaway speed.*

So if you're thinking what I'm thinking, then you must also be thinking, *So why on earth does Victor need the world's fastest snout?*

This is very good thinking on your part, and, to be honest, I need a moment to think about the answer. Besides, all that talk of chocolate has made me hungry. I'll just be a minute or two.

While I'm away, here's a maze for you to solve:

WHO WILL GET THE WORM FIRST, ROSALIE OR VICTOR?

TIP: Why not use a pencil, so if you go wrong or want to do it again, you can easily erase?

NOTE: If this is a library book, **_PLEASE DON'T DRAW ON THIS PAGE!_**
Your librarian won't like that one little bit.

FASTER THAN A SPEEDING . . . GRUB?

OKAY. I'M BACK. I'VE EATEN FOUR CHOCOLATES, and I've got a few theories about Victor's nose.

THEORY A: Victor uses his snout fingers to tickle bugs out of hiding. Maybe bugs are smart enough to lie still if they are poked once. But even bugs will wiggle and giggle if you tickle them at supersonic speeds with twenty-two snout fingers.

THEORY B: Victor's star looks a lot like twenty-two worms. When a worm sees Victor's snout, it thinks its family has come for a visit and pops its head out to say hello.

THEORY C (NOT MY IDEA): Because Victor's nose moves so fast, he is able to find and eat the tiniest grubs that wouldn't be worth the effort to find and eat unless it took only 0.12 seconds. The mud is crawling with bitsy bugs, but Victor needs hundreds to get a full belly. Only a supersonic snout can get the job done! Also, Victor's two front teeth are like tweezers and can pluck tiny larvae from the mud.

These are all very good theories, but they all have their problems. The problem with theory A is that bugs aren't ticklish. The problem with theory B is that worms don't have eyes and can't recognize their family. And the problem with theory C is that these larvae are too small to see without my magnifying glass. And I can't find my magnifying glass. But theory C is probably the right one.

Okay. Time to get back to Rosalie. I bet she's getting hungry. But before we go, Victor's snout has one more trick. Victor can smell underwater! With nostril bubbles! While Victor is swimming, he blows bubbles out of his nostrils, then inhales them back in. The bubbles pick up smells from anything they touch, which lets Victor know if anything tasty is swimming around. I'd like to see Superman try that!

HUNGRY, HUNGRY MOLE

YES, ROSALIE IS HUNGRY NOW. But Rosalie is usually hungry. Moles eat a lot! Rosalie scampers a mile or two each day. And don't forget all that digging. Hungry work!

Rosalie might look like a spongy potato, but she is actually very fit and lean. She has only enough body fat to survive three days without food. Which means Rosalie needs to get her worms, and on time!

To keep herself in tiptop shape, Rosalie eats at least 70 percent of her body weight each day, or probably well over a hundred worms. That's a lot! And that's why moles are constantly patrolling their tunnels. In fact, worms are the whole reason moles dig.

You see, tunnels are like giant spiderwebs for catching worms. If a worm wriggles too close to a tunnel, it might crawl through the wall and fall in. Bad move, worm! Rosalie's **EARLY WHISKER WARNING SYSTEM** lets her know something tasty has arrived, and off she scampers to investigate.

FIRST, she pokes the worm with her snout finger, just to make sure it's a worm.

THEN, she holds it between her claws and squeezes to clean out the worm's gut-grit.

FINALLY, she tears off big worm chunks with her sharp little teeth. Yum-yum!

If she can't find enough worms in her main highways, she might dig a just-below-the-surface tunnel. These sometimes collapse as soon as Rosalie digs them, but worms like to hang out in loose garden soil.

But here's a worry. What if a cold snap hits, the worms freeze, and the ground is too hard to dig? Or what if a heat wave shrivels all the worms like fried onions? Or what if a wormhole sucks all the worms into outer space? Trouble! Three days without worms, and that's the end of Rosalie. But not to fear! Rosalie is always one step ahead of the weather and the worms (but probably not the wormholes).

SEE THOSE WPs ON THE PLAN OF ROSALIE'S HOME? Those are Rosalie's worm pantries. If Rosalie finds more worms than she can eat, she stores them in a special room, just like how you store extra cans of beans in a special pantry cupboard.

It's a very sensible plan. But worms don't like sensible plans. Any worm worth its wriggle would crawl away through the pantry walls. And Rosalie can't store dead worms because worms are really only dirt and water, which means they decompose faster than you can say "Why wandering worms wonder why worms wander."

So how does Rosalie keep her pantry worms from escaping?

SHE BITES OFF THEIR HEADS!

Now, that would be the end for you or me, but not for worms. A worm can grow a new head in a couple of months. But until it gets a new head, it can't move, which is just the way Rosalie likes it. Sometimes she stores hundreds of worms in a pantry. Sometimes she just pats a few into the walls of her tunnels. Those are the wriggly **WW** lines on the map. Gross, right? But also pretty darn crafty.

SUPERPOWER #9

SALIVA OF DEATH (MAYBE?)

RUMOR HAS IT THAT ROSALIE HAS TOXIC SALIVA that stuns worms. (I don't think it is powerful enough to hurt you, but still—I'd avoid getting bitten by a mole. A mole has forty-four very sharp teeth.) Moles do have large saliva glands, but is their spit toxic? I'm going to say yes, but I can't seem to get a straight answer on this. Which leads me to an important point about moles: **MOLES ARE INSCRUTABLE.**

SALIVA OF DEATH

STARRING ROSALIE THE MOLE

NOW SHOWING

"DOUBLE BILL"
SALIVA OF DEATH
GREAT MOLE MYSTERY
7 PM

Inscrutable is a fancy way of saying "very hard to see." But *inscrutable* also means somewhat mysterious, even a bit unknowable. Why are your left socks always missing? Where does the Easter Bunny live? These things are inscrutable, just like moles.

Even scientists don't know exactly what moles do down there, because they can't see down there. Nobody aboveground can really see what's going on underground without digging up the moles' tunnels.

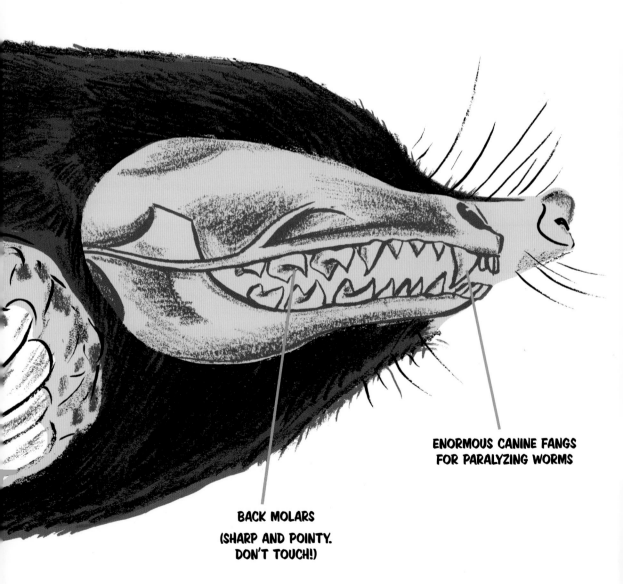

ENORMOUS CANINE FANGS
FOR PARALYZING WORMS

BACK MOLARS

(SHARP AND POINTY.
DON'T TOUCH!)

Some scientists have put radio transmitters on moles to follow their movements underground. Other scientists have driven radar machines aboveground to map underground tunnel systems. Scientists also study moles in fake laboratory tunnels, but laboratory moles don't act the same as wild moles. Only when scientists can shrink themselves to fit into mole tunnels will they truly understand what moles do down there. But then, the moles might think the scientists were worms, and that would be trouble.

In any case, what I'm trying to say is that scientists know a lot about moles, but not everything. Great mole mysteries are still waiting to be solved . . . perhaps by you.

And on that note, **TIME FOR YOUR NEXT QUIZ.**

QUIZ #2

PLEASE ANSWER TRUE OR FALSE.

1. Victor's snout fingers move so fast they sometimes burst into flames. That's why he lives close to water.

2. Rosalie has an army of headless zombie worms.

3. The best way to catch a mole is to stick your finger in a molehill and wait until the mole bites.

4. Moles swim across oceans using nostril bubbles as water wings.

5. Rosalie scampers clockwise through her tunnels so she doesn't rub her fur the wrong way with dirt.

ANSWERS:

1. **FALSE.** Snout flames? That's ridiculous! But Victor's nose does work hard enough to get little blisters and sore spots. And that's why Victor prefers wet and boggy places—they're softer on his nose.

2. **FALSE.** Another ridiculous question. Zombies always have heads.

3. **FALSE.** Who wrote this quiz? Never stick your finger in a molehill! A mole probably won't bite your finger, but I wouldn't chance it.

4. **FALSE.** No mole could swim across an ocean, but all moles do swim well with the help of bubbles. Their thick fur traps air bubbles (not nostril bubbles), which help moles float.

5. **FALSE.** Mole fur is very dense and very short, and (most important) it's reversible, which means it never rubs the wrong way, like your cat's fur does. That means mole fur lies the right way whether moles are going backwards or forward. And that's a good thing for animals living in tight, dirty tunnels. And here's an extra piece of mole trivia: Mole fur is always beautifully clean despite all that dirt. Dirt just doesn't seem to stick to mole fur. Nobody knows why. Inscrutable!

LIFE UNDERGROUND

YOU KNOW A LOT ABOUT ROSALIE NOW. You know what she eats and where she stores her worms. You know she's stronger than Hercules and squishier than a potato. But I haven't told you much about her life underground.

Some moles like leaving their tunnels. Victor does. He loves to swim. So do desmans. The shrew moles also spend time snuffling around the leaves on the forest floor. Scientists call these moles *semi-fossorial. Semi* means "half" and *fossorial* is just a fancy word for "digger," so semi-fossorial moles are part-time diggers—they like to see something other than dirt. But Rosalie is 100 percent *fossorial*, which means *she spends her entire life underground!* She doesn't even have a door to the aboveground world.

Don't believe me? Look back to the map of Rosalie's home. Do you see a front door or a back door or any other kind of door? There isn't one! (Remember, lateral shafts and molehills are just dirt-dumping ditches, not escape routes.) If Rosalie ever wanted to leave her home, she would have to dig a new tunnel to the surface!

Now, an entire life spent underground is very different than your life. Because Rosalie can't see the sun or the moon, she doesn't know daytime from nighttime, which means Rosalie doesn't live by the same clock as you. Instead of your twenty-four-hour day, she prefers eight-hour shifts. She scampers, eats, and digs for about four hours, then she sleeps for about four hours. Then back to scampering, eating, and digging.

In other words, Rosalie organizes her time just as she pleases. In fact, everything in Rosalie's world is just as she pleases. Rosalie lives, eats, digs, sleeps, and poops just as she pleases. You might say (and I certainly do) that Rosalie has created her very own private universe, or what I like to call **MOLETOPIA.**

MOLETOPIA

WHEN PEOPLE TALK ABOUT *UTOPIA*, they mean the best place on earth, for them. Your utopia might be a place where the trees are made out of Legos and the dog can do your homework. In my utopia, my pencils are always sharp and my closest friends are monkeys. Utopias are usually dreamy places that we never quite reach. But Rosalie is a doer, not a dreamer. She went ahead and built her utopia.

In Moletopia, scrumptious worm dinners just drop through the ceiling. In Moletopia, worm candies are hidden in the walls. In Moletopia, everything is connected by custom-built hallways. Most animals have to leave their homes to find dinner or stretch their legs. But not Rosalie. Imagine if the grocery store, your favorite pizzeria, and the park were all connected to your bedroom by cozy passageways. You'd never need to go outside, so you'd never need a coat, even in winter.

And speaking of winter, some animals have to grow thick fur or worry about finding enough food when the world is frozen and cold. But not Rosalie. Rosalie even has a thermostat of sorts. If the soil freezes in winter or gets too hot in summer, she follows the worms into deeper tunnels, where the temperature is more pleasant.

Moles don't even go aboveground to find a mate. Every spring, male moles tunnel toward the nearest ladies. How they know where to find them is a mystery, but you'll always know a mole has been beelining toward a lady because his molehills follow his perfectly straight tunnel. (Usually, mole tunnels are more winding and random.)

But the very best part of Moletopia is that other animals don't know it exists. Owls, foxes, badgers, and pretty much all creatures that think moles are tasty treats don't know moles are even down there. Moles live far enough underground that predators can't smell them. And moles don't have front doors, so nobody can come knocking. A very hungry weasel might burrow down a molehill, and digging just-below-the-surface tunnels can be dangerous because animals can see moles digging. But most of the time, a mole is as safe as a peanut in a shell. Moletopia is so scrumdiddlyumptious, Rosalie never, ever leaves unless one of the Terrible Four happens.

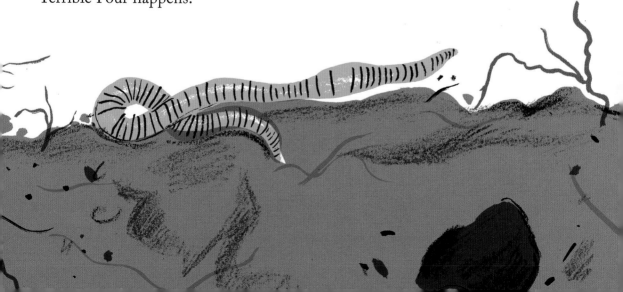

THE TERRIBLE FOUR

TERRIBLE ONE: Rosalie needs fresh grasses for bedding. (A dirty bed isn't truly terrible, but it isn't very nice either.)

TERRIBLE TWO: A rainstorm has flooded her tunnels and her fortress has collapsed!

TERRIBLE THREE: The summer is so hot, Rosalie needs water! Since worms are 80 percent water, Rosalie usually doesn't drink (which also means she usually doesn't pee). But during bad droughts, when even the worms are thirsty, Rosalie may need to find a stream.

TERRIBLE FOUR: Her mother kicked her out . . . aboveground! Now, most animals eventually leave home to start their own lives. But Rosalie and her two brothers and one sister were only two months old when they were sent up and out. They couldn't tell a pinecone from a polecat, and they had to scurry blindly along the forest floor. Help! Scary!

Scientists call this the *juvenile dispersal.* But I call it the **DANGEROUS OVERLAND SCAMPER.** It's a very bad time to be a mole, but a very good time to be an owl or a fox, if you know what I mean. Half the moles don't survive.

At two years old, Rosalie is a middle-aged mole. Most moles don't live more than four years in the wild.

But Rosalie was lucky. She found her grandfather's abandoned home about a mile away. She had to repair a few tumbled tunnels and dig some new ones. But now, Rosalie is super-fantastically safe and cozy in her very own Moletopia.

HOME, DEADLY HOME

ROSALIE MAY LOVE HER HOME, but Moletopia wouldn't suit me at all. I wouldn't like to live underground and never see the sun or the moon. I'd get lonely without my family. And I don't like worms. But worse, Moletopia could kill me!

To understand why, we're going to need a short biology lesson.

I'm sorry to leave such a heavy subject until the end, because—let's be honest—you're probably a bit tired by now. I know I am. So you can stop reading here . . .

You're still reading?

Yay! I know I said I wouldn't mind if you stopped, but I'm very glad you're still here. I'll make this as short and pleasant as possible.

You might already know that animals need *oxygen* to survive. Oxygen is an invisible gas—think of it as tiny bubbles floating about in the air. (Scientists call these oxygen bubbles *molecules*.)

When we breathe air in, we breathe oxygen in. Blood flows through our lung tissues, picks up the oxygen, and carries it to every corner and cranny of our bodies. It's oxygen (and food) that keeps our bodies working well.

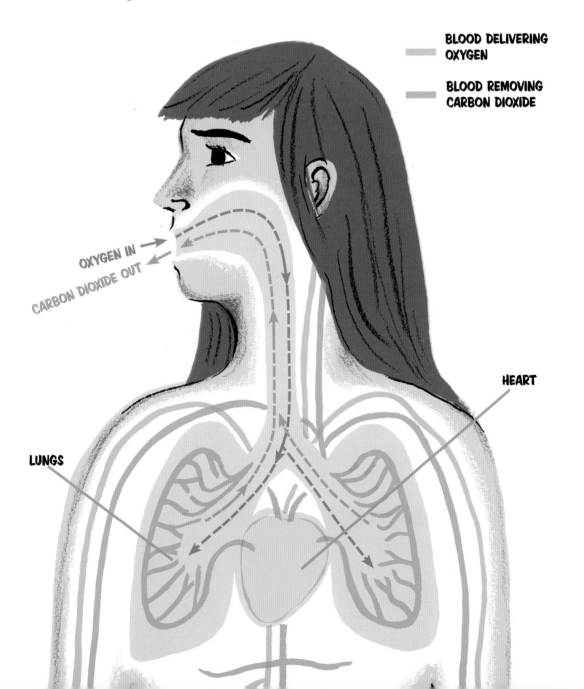

BLOOD DELIVERING OXYGEN

BLOOD REMOVING CARBON DIOXIDE

OXYGEN IN →
← CARBON DIOXIDE OUT

HEART

LUNGS

The stronger and harder our bodies work, the more oxygen we need and the harder and faster we breathe. That's because muscles need much more oxygen to run or jump or dig than they do to sit and read this book.

And, of course, we don't just breathe in. We also breathe out. Every time we breathe out, our bodies get rid of a gas called *carbon dioxide.* Think of carbon dioxide as your body's exhaust fumes. Dump trucks belch black smoke from their engines, and you belch carbon dioxide.

So far, so good?

Now, fresh air is about 21 percent oxygen and 0.04 percent carbon dioxide. So if gases are like bubbles, one of every five bubbles floating about in the air is oxygen. And one in twenty-five hundred bubbles is carbon dioxide. (The rest of air is other stuff that we won't worry about.)

And that's how most animals like their air. But if the number of oxygen bubbles goes down or the number of carbon dioxide bubbles goes up, that's big trouble!

Imagine stepping inside a tube that seals shut behind you. When you first step in, the air inside will have 21 percent oxygen and 0.04 percent carbon dioxide, just like fresh air. But as you breathe in and out, in and out, in and out, the bubbles in the air will gradually change. As you breathe oxygen into your body, there will be fewer oxygen bubbles inside the tube. And as you breathe carbon dioxide out, there will be more and more carbon dioxide bubbles. After a while, your body isn't going to like being inside that tube. Not one little bit.

As the oxygen drops, you'll start getting woozy. Very soon your arms will feel too heavy to lift, because your muscles won't have the oxygen they need to work. You'll turn purple. You'll start gasping for air. When the oxygen level hits 10 percent, you'll pass out.

The same nasty business happens as carbon dioxide rises each time you breathe out. Remember, carbon dioxide is your body's exhaust fumes—you're stuck in a tube breathing your own fumes! When carbon dioxide reaches 1 percent, you'll become drowsy and start breathing rapidly. As carbon dioxide rises, you'll get confused and dizzy. Your eyes, nose, and lungs will burn. And if you stay in that tube until the carbon dioxide level reaches 5 percent, you'll pass out. If you don't get back to fresh air, you'll die.

Now, who lives in a tube with no doors or windows and no fresh air? Rosalie! Scientists tested a mole tunnel and discovered the air was 14.3 percent oxygen and 5.5 percent carbon dioxide! Another mole tunnel had only 7 percent oxygen. Awful and horrible—for a human. But just an ordinary day in Moletopia.

And as you know, moles don't just sit around reading books. They dig and push and sweat. Think of Hercules trying to lift those eight bulls. And now imagine him lifting even one bull while breathing the air in Rosalie's tunnels. Impossible!

So how does Rosalie do it?

The high levels of carbon dioxide in Rosalie's tunnels aren't just from her own breathing. Tiny **microbes** in the soil belch out tons of carbon dioxide, and they gobble up lots of oxygen too.

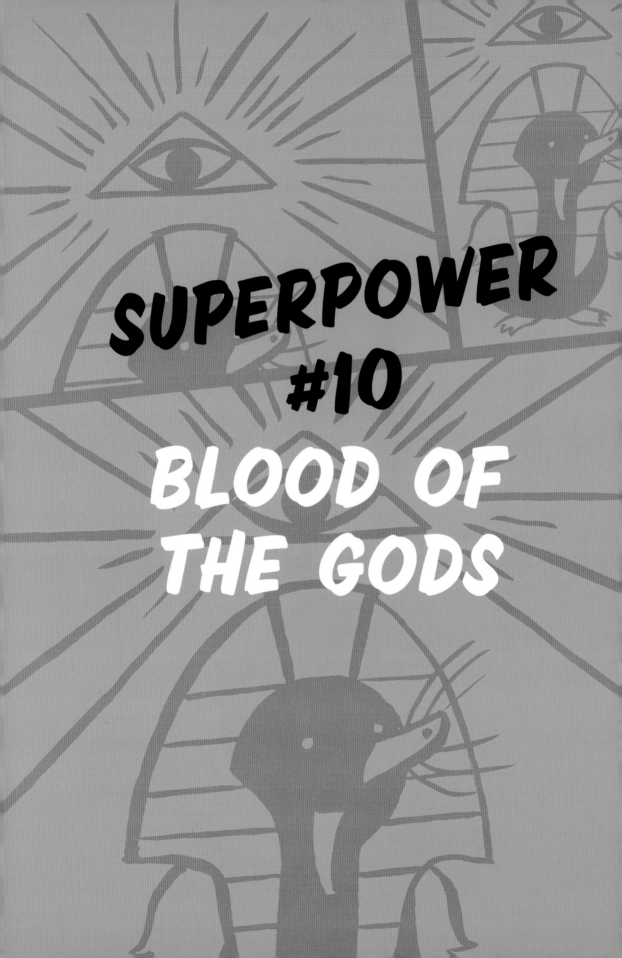

SUPERPOWER #10

BLOOD OF THE GODS

YOU ALREADY KNOW THAT BLOOD flows to your lungs, picks up oxygen, and carries it to all parts of your body. Now imagine your blood as a roller coaster speeding around your body. Riding that roller coaster are millions of tiny people, and it's their job to grab oxygen as they zoom past your lungs.

When your lungs are filled with oxygen, it's easy for everyone to grab an oxygen bubble as they all whiz past. But when there are fewer oxygen bubbles available, not everyone can find and grab one quickly enough before the roller coaster rolls on by. Then, as the coaster continues traveling around your body, there simply isn't enough oxygen to go around. And hard-working muscles and organs won't have enough oxygen to do their jobs.

That's when bad things happen to you or me, but it's also when Rosalie shows her inner superhero. You see, the little people riding around in Rosalie's blood have *powers*.

If you know *Star Wars,* you'll know that Luke Skywalker can use the Force to pull anything toward him. And if you know superheroes, you'll know that the Viking god Thor can command his hammer—no matter where

Your blood is made up of several different parts. It's your **red blood cells** that transport oxygen around your body. Red blood cells contain a very important thing called **hemoglobin.** It's the hemoglobin that grabs oxygen from your lungs. So imagine your red blood cells as the roller-coaster cars and the hemoglobin as the tiny people.

it is—to fly into his hand. Well, Rosalie's blood has the same sort of power over oxygen. Scientists call it *high oxygen affinity.* I say she has the **BLOOD OF THE GODS!**

Now, to be perfectly clear, there are no tiny Viking gods riding around in Rosalie's blood. But if there were, you can imagine how good they'd be at collecting oxygen. As they whizzed past Rosalie's lungs, the tiny Thors would command every last oxygen molecule to jump in the roller coaster before it zoomed away again. And that's precisely what high oxygen affinity means. It means that Rosalie's blood will find any oxygen molecules—no matter how few and far between—and hold on tight.

But that's not all. You can't have the **BLOOD OF THE GODS** running in your veins without being extra-special on the inside. And believe me, Rosalie's insides are so extra-special, scientists aren't even sure how they work.

INTRODUCING ROSALIE:

BIONIC BURROWER!

SCIENTISTS DON'T UNDERSTAND ALL THE WAYS that Rosalie survives underground, but they do know a few important things.

First, Rosalie has special networks of tight blood vessels that help quickly pop the super-stuck oxygen out where it's needed. She has great big lungs, which means more oxygen can get into her lungs with every breath. She also has more blood than normal, and more blood means more tiny Thors commanding more oxygen. Rosalie also has supersize muscles that actually store oxygen right inside themselves—when her muscles are hard at work, they have their own secret stash of oxygen to help them keep working strong.

And those are just a few ways Rosalie survives low oxygen. Remember, she also has to survive horribly high carbon dioxide.

Animals that live high in the mountains where the air is thin (like llamas in the Andes) or super-high-flying birds (like bar-headed geese that soar over the Himalayas) can also survive low oxygen. But it's only the amazing *subterranean* folks like Rosalie who survive low oxygen *and* high carbon dioxide. And she does it all with the grace of a swimmer and the brute force of a backhoe. That's what I call a **BIONIC BURROWER!**

Scientists are even studying mole blood in the hopes of designing a **SUPERBLOOD** to help people who are sick and need blood transfusions or new organs. Rosalie's blood might even hold secrets to help people with lung disease. Who knows what wondrous mole mysteries will be uncovered next!

But if you think Rosalie is remarkable, you should hear my story about **ENO THE OSTRICH, SUPERSONIC SURVIVOR!**

GLOSSARY

CARBON DIOXIDE: Carbon dioxide is one of the gassy building blocks of our world. It is what you breathe out and what plants breathe in.

CYLINDRICAL (see-lynn-dree-cal): Shaped like a potato in a tube.

EIMER'S ORGANS (I-mers or-gans): Very, very sensitive tiny bumps on mole noses.

FORTRESS: An enormous mound of dirt built by some moles for reasons not yet fully understood.

FOSSORIAL: An animal that digs for a living.

GRUBS: Legless, wormlike baby bugs and beetles. Also known as larvae.

HEMOGLOBIN (he-mo-glow-bin): A molecule that picks up oxygen in your lungs and carries it to all parts of your body.

HIGH OXYGEN AFFINITY: The talent of being able to find and grab oxygen even when there is very little oxygen to find and grab.

HUMERUS (hew-mer-us): The upper arm bone.

JUVENILE DISPERSAL: A very bad time to be a young mole.

LATRINE: A toilet, also known as a lavatory, a water closet, the potty, and the loo.

MICROBES: Itsy-bitsy living things, like bacteria. You need a very good microscope to see them.

MOLECULES: Molecules are really more like building blocks than bubbles— everything in the entire world is made out of them, but they are so very, very, very small, you won't see them until you're a famous scientist with a superpowered microscope.

MOULDYWARP: Old English for "He Who Hurls the Earth."

OPPOSABLE: A thumb that can touch other fingers. It lets people, primates, and a few other animals grasp things with their hands.

OXYGEN: You can't see it, but it's all around you, and you need to breathe it to survive.

PREPOLLEX: Long, curvy bone that grows from a mole's wrist alongside a mole's re
thumb.

RED BLOOD CELLS: Most of your blood is made up of these. Other parts of your
blood are white blood cells, plasma, and platelets.

SEMI-FOSSORIAL: Part-time digger.

SUBTERRANEAN (sub-ter-rain-knee-an): Anyone who lives underground.

UTOPIA (you-toe-pee-ah): The best place on earth.

FURTHER MOLE READING

Mighty Mole and Super Soil by Mary Quattlebaum (Dawn Publications, 2016)

Star-Nosed Moles by Marcia Zappa (Abdo, 2016)

IF YOU'RE FEELING COURAGEOUS:

Moles by Rob Atkinson (Whittet Books, 2013)

IF YOU'RE FEELING VERY, VERY COURAGEOUS:

The Natural History of Moles by Martyn Gorman and R. David Stone (Cornell
    University Press, 1990)

AND NO LIST OF MOLE BOOKS WOULD BE COMPLETE WITHOUT:

The Wind in the Willows by Kenneth Grahame (first published in 1908)
    The character Mole is a common European mole, just like Rosalie. But remember,
    moles do not eat cold chicken or fried ham and they rarely wear slippers.

FOR MORE MOLE FACTS ONLINE:

BBC NATURE: Want to watch the ultimate digging machine in action? Check out the
    video at www.bbc.co.uk/programmes/p01f9lwf.

WORLD'S DEADLIEST: Could star-nosed moles have the deadliest noses on the planet?
    See video.nationalgeographic.com/video/worlds-deadliest-ngs/deadliest-star-
    nosed-mole.